Monsters

Written and illustrated by
Steve Smallman

Collins *Educational*
An imprint of HarperCollins*Publishers*

A small monster.

A hairy monster.

A scary monster.

A blue monster.

A glue monster.

A crying monster.

A wet monster.

A pet monster.

A loud monster.

A jelly monster.

A smelly monster.

A big, fat belly monster.